IMAGES
of America

ROCHESTER'S
LAKESIDE RESORTS
AND AMUSEMENT PARKS

The red and green pin-back button was given out to promote the park's "grand opening" on June 4, 1906. It marked the amusement park's 22nd season.

IMAGES
of America

ROCHESTER'S
LAKESIDE RESORTS
AND AMUSEMENT PARKS

Donovan A. Shilling

ARCADIA

First published 1999
Reprinted 2000, 2001, 2003, 2004

Published by Arcadia Publishing,
Charleston SC, Chicago IL, Portsmouth NH, San Francisco CA

Printed in Great Britain

Library of Congress Catalog Card Number: 99-62640

For all general information, contact Arcadia Publishing:
Telephone 843-853-2070
Fax 843-853-0044
E-mail sales@arcadiapublishing.com
For customer service and orders:
Toll-free 1-888-313-2665

Visit us on the Internet at www.arcadiapublishing.com

*This book is dedicated to the memory of all those who once enjoyed
Rochester's wonderful resorts and to my grandchildren:
Morgan, Jonas, Madeline, Alexander, and Katrina.
May they someday appreciate the rich history of this region as I have.*

CONTENTS

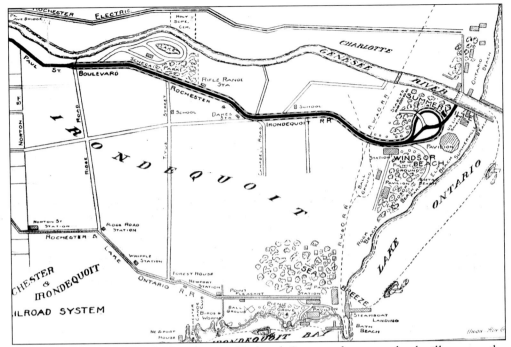

Issued by the Rochester & Irondequoit Railroad System, the map clearly illustrates the locations of six lake and bay-side resorts and their geographical relationship to one another. Not shown is White City, situated west of Rock Beach and Glen Haven Park, south of the Newport House. All resorts had a picnic grove and pavilion, a baseball diamond, and a bathing beach. Larger resorts offered stables, boat rental, a hotel and restaurant, and boat landing. The trolley company advertised that its cars were "open, clean, and filled with Ontario's ozone-laden air."

> *To stay in town these red hot days,*
> *To say the least is tough;*
> *So take a car to Windsor Beach*
> *And lunch upon the bluff.*

> *Come, boys and girls of every age,*
> *Get ready for a lark,*
> *And take a trolley ride with me*
> *To Sea Breeze Park.*

INTRODUCTION

At one time, Rochester, New York, was favored with more than two dozen lake and bay-side resorts whose grand hotels served a tidal wave of summer guests. The resorts might be thought of as "tinsel meccas on the golden shore." Families swept happily onto the sandy beaches of Lake Ontario, and sportsmen gathered eagerly along the reedy shorelines of Irondequoit Bay. For 50 years, between 1870 and 1920, train loads, boat loads, and jam-packed trolleys conveyed vacationers and conventioneers out of the steamy cities of Pittsburgh, Philadelphia, Buffalo, Syracuse, and Rochester.

Others came from smaller towns, villages, and hamlets in Pennsylvania and New York. All sought respite from the humid days of summer when air conditioning was done with a hand-held paper fan. Vacationers looked forward to a week or more of shore dinners, fishing, relaxation, and, above all, the cool off-shore and on-shore breezes that are seldom enjoyed in inland countryside.

Behind their love for the lakeside and fanaticism for fishing, there was a strong Victorian conviction that returning to nature brought one closer to the Almighty. Each resort area had its bathing area, picnic grove, baseball diamond, shady paths, gardens, and fishing facilities often with boats and canoes for rent. Hotels offered wide verandas complete with rocking chairs, gliders, and hammocks.

The tinsel meccas began at Manitou Beach and its amusement park on the west. Going east one encountered Grand View Beach, Crescent Beach, and Island Cottage. At Charlotte and Ontario Beach Park almost a dozen hotels blossomed to serve the public. Literally thousands of fun seekers were brought by the New York Central & Hudson River Railroad to daily, weekly, and month-long stays at the area resorts and amusement parks. Later, trolley lines conveyed the masses to these vacation spots.

Farther eastward, across the Genesee River, was Summerville, Windsor Beach, and that remarkable tent community called White City. Beyond, small steamers took the crowds on a 5-mile trip to Sea Breeze on bonny Irondequoit Bay. It too had its restaurants, picnic groves, and pavilions. A naphtha launch ride on the bay then transported others to a continuous line of small cottages, hotels, and private clubs.

Vessels called the *Galusha*, the *Woodworth*, the *Lookout*, and the *Glen Edyth* delivered gatherings to Point Pleasant, Birds and Worms, Glen Edyth, and the fabled Newport House. However, the magnet for many was the cool shade of Glen Haven with its gracious grounds, hotels, flower-lined pathways, and delightful amusement parks. The Royal Blue Line provided the trolley return to Rochester from this rich and wonderful assortment of tinsel meccas that once sparkled like gems on Lake Ontario and Irondequoit Bay's golden shores.

It is the writer's hope that these images of the past will rekindle interest in those marvelous days of yesteryear when so many found delight in our exceptional water-side resources.

Thanks go to Russ Leo, Jim Dierks, Pat Wayne, Alan Mueller, Lorraine Bean, and the Rochester Chapter of the National Railway Historical Society for their assistance in providing some of the rare photographs in this book. A special thank you to my wife, Yolanda, who supported me in this project.

—Donovan A. Shilling, February 1999

One

Ontario Beach Park

The three-story Hotel Ontario, the largest hostelry on Lake Ontario, was a magnificent example of Victorian, Queen Anne-style architecture. The hotel offered scores of rooms for vacationing guests at Ontario Beach and catered to the palates of the thousands that descended on the park grounds on weekends. Its wide upper and lower verandas were frequently crowded with patrons enjoying trout, jack perch, or freshly caught Lake Ontario white fish dinners. For years a reservation was needed to either stay or dine at the impressive hotel.

Scene at Ontario Beach.   Rochester, N. Y.

Fire destroyed the 73-room Spencer House, a favorite summer retreat for Rochester, New York citizens, in 1882. Its location on Lake Ontario, at the point where the Genesee River flows into the lake, made it a desirable resort site. In 1883 the New York Central & Hudson River R.R. purchased the lake front site at a sheriff's sale. They then leased the property, creating the Ontario Beach Improvement Company. As private promoters built an expansive hotel, the rail line constructed a balloon-shaped track on the grounds to attract picnickers.

2463—Ontario Beach Park, Rochester, N. Y.

The grand opening of Ontario Beach Park took place on Saturday, August 2, 1884. Twelve thousand curious citizens crowded into the showy new playground, mostly by train. They found a promenade along the shore cleared, flowers and grassy areas planted, fountains installed, and walkways laid out for their convenience. Each of the eight rail coaches carried up to 100 passengers. Weekend excursion trains filled the park with thousands from as far away as Ohio, Pennsylvania, and New Jersey.

Main Entrance, Ontario Beach Park, N. Y.

On July 3, 1889, an electric railway, the first in Rochester, began operation from Wagg's Corners (West Ridge Road) down the Boulevard (Lake Avenue) to the amusement park. Trolley fare was 5¢. The railroad met the challenge by building a high-board fence around its park, charging trolley riders 10¢ admission. Park admission, however, was free to excursion train riders. Note the Moorish-style main entrance.

5991. Entrance, Ontario Beach Park, Charlotte, N. Y.

To accommodate the crowds, a second entrance to Ontario Beach Park was opened on the southeast side of Beach Avenue in Charlotte, New York. Few men in summer were without their favorite straw hats or "skimmers," while ladies wore long, ground-sweeping shirts, fluffy white blouses, and large, feathered hats. Note the addition of electric lights to the entrance arch.

2466—A Summer Afternoon at Ontario Beach Park, Rochester, N. Y.

Warm summer Sundays brought vast crowds seeking the delights offered by the tinsel mecca on Ontario's shore. By the late 1890s, the glittering amusement park had gained a new title, "The Coney Island of Western New York." Note that ladies carried large silk parasols for shade, not for protection from rain. After strolling the boardwalk and midway, visitors rested on convenient wooden benches.

Lake waters often lapped at the boardwalk's edge. A simple rail fence separated park goers from the lake. While no one swam, a few youngsters waded in the sand. For nighttime illumination, arc lights were supported by tall poles while strings of colored lights were suspended between the poles.

5986. Bathing Beach, Charlotte, N. Y.

Lake Ontario's shoreline was never constant. A series of four large platforms were built with benches sporting heart-shaped sides to accommodate sightseers. As of yet, there was no wooden "boardwalk." A "terrace" of packed sand provided the pathway along the shore.

VIEW OF ONTANO BEACH PARK, ROCHESTER, N. Y.

By 1905 an impressive framework of massive timbers spanned the lake front boardwalk. The colonnade was decorated with red, white, and blue patriotic variations of the American flag. Gay banners snapped and fluttered in lake breezes, adding a festive air to the shoreline. Victorian fun seekers boarded the "Circle Swing," a tall, chair-swing ride that dominated the skyline.

13

A view from Lake Ontario reveals a small part of Ontario Beach Park's festive amusement area. This 1909 view shows the lake's high water level that year.

This is the largest hotel at the lake where
They serve fine dinners.

Opening in 1884, the Hotel Ontario was both an elegant and practical example of Victorian enterprise. On its extensive, shady lower verandas and its sunlit upper porches, great gatherings of summer convention goers and train excursionists enjoyed fare served by uniformed, white-gloved waiters. Shore dinners included delicious roast chicken, whitefish and trout, oyster stew, or clam chowder followed, perhaps, by a generous schooner of Bartholomay's famous beer.

14

A wide midway was located beyond the park's entrance. Bordering it were dozens of attractions including games of chance, rides, and refreshment stands offering a variety of summertime specials. Popcorn, peanuts, candy apples, lemonade, and ice cream were everyone's favorites. However, the Ottman Brothers offered something unique—Coney Island Hots.

Some visitors sought the park's shady benches. Others were drawn to attractions such as Chubbuck's Wheel Swing. The wheel spun patrons on a revolving ride at a modest speed. To many whose lives were quite uneventful, the experience was both rare and exciting. Such rides often became a happy topic of conversation long after the park trip was over.

What better way to spend a Sunday in 1905 than to take a B.R. & P. rail excursion to Ontario Beach Park? Even if one lived as far away as Pennsylvania, the Buffalo, Rochester &Pittsburgh Railway could get you there in plenty of time to enjoy the day. The special excursion train was scheduled to leave the park at 7 p.m. Fares included admission to the park.

Alert to the latest craze, the park offered visitors an "Automatic Vaudeville." For "only 1¢," one operated a crank on a device that rotated a series of pictures affixed to a wheel. Rapid turning of the wheel gave viewers an illusion of motion as the pictures flashed by. The penny spent produced a pretty girl dancing, a horse racing, or a prizefighter boxing. The sign in the arcade entrance refers to E.B. Moore's photographic booth. Visitors could have their pictures taken and made part of a mailable postcard.

The park's western side was dominated by a popular ride called the "Virginia Reel." Two stories high, it took thrill seekers on a looping ride in a rail car that rolled first back and forth then round and round in ever smaller circles until coasting to a sudden stop at the bottom of its artificial hill.

The park's eastern edge accommodated L.A. Thompson's "Scenic Railway." At first called the "Russian Railway," the gentle roller coaster ride later became the much loved "Breezer." In a string of connected cars, 20 riders experienced a variety of dips and turns finally looping back through a darkened tunnel where fake lions and tigers growled loudly. The sound effects added to the fun and brought shrieks from both young and old.

The auditorium on the left hosted many themes. The sign announced "OUT OF THE NORTH." Within the building, a group of genuine Canadian native people were on display. Called "Esquimouix," they dressed in native costume. Perhaps they were well paid to endure the summer's heat in their furry garb. Later, the auditorium became the "House of Hilarity," offering vaudeville.

A Ferris wheel and the Scenic Railway brought new thrills to many who flocked to the park. On opening day 1907, a record attendance was set. Some 42,000 sightseers, eager to enjoy the added attractions and improvements, jammed into Ontario Beach Park to be "enchanted by the erection of a magic city." Promoters billed the park as "Wizard-ville by the Lake."

PONY TRACK, ONTARIO BEACH, N. Y.

Published by L. J. Sexton, Ontario Beach, N. Y. *this is where I spent some of my time Sun. 22. Mas Belle Barnes*

In an era when "Old Dobbin" was a common means of transportation, kids were thrilled to ride a pony, a horse, or even a mule around the track. In 1906 kids loved to ride "Maud," a fine looking mare that gave children a memorable ride.

Another view shows the large, double pony track at the lower right behind the promenade fence. The Ontario Beach Hotel and Auditorium Theater in the background fly 44-star American flags.

19

Band Stand,
Ontario Beach Park,
Port of Rochester, N. Y.

A handsome, three-story bandshell was located opposite the park's Ontario Hotel. Throngs gathered on lakeside benches to hear grand Sunday concerts. Musical groups included military units such as the 54th Regiment Band and Lapham's Red Hussars. On August 24, 1894, the evening concert was followed by "the event of the season," produced by "$1000.00 in FIREWORKS!" Pyrotechnics included "500 rockets, 10,000 fiery dragons, and a million stars."

An August 5, 1917 Sunday band concert brought a host of music lovers to Ontario Beach Park's colorful bandshell. The flag was illuminated with electric lights when patriotic marches were played. (Photo courtesy of Greece Historical Society.)

On May 30, 1892, Pres. Benjamin Harrison came to Rochester, New York, to dedicate the Soldiers and Sailors Monument in Washington Square. State Gov. Roswell P. Flower and Mayor Richard A. Curran were also in attendance. Prior to the monument's unveiling, the President, governor, and other dignitaries rode the street railway's "Palace Car" to Ontario Beach. The Wheelmen's League, their bicycles bedecked in flags, escorted the President to Bartholomay's Cottage Hotel for a grand breakfast.

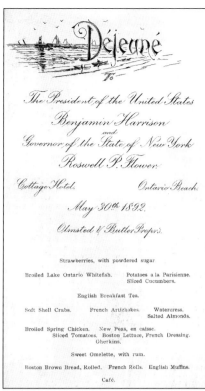

Déjeuné
To
The President of the United States
Benjamin Harrison
and
Governor of the State of New York
Roswell P. Flower

Cottage Hotel.   Ontario Beach.

May 30th 1892.

Olmsted & Butler Proprs.

Strawberries, with powdered sugar

Broiled Lake Ontario Whitefish.   Potatoes a la Parisienne.
                                   Sliced Cucumbers.

English Breakfast Tea.

Soft Shell Crabs.   French Artichokes.   Watercress.
                                           Salted Almonds.

Broiled Spring Chicken.   New Peas, en caisse.
         Sliced Tomatoes. Boston Lettuce, French Dressing.
                           Gherkins.

Sweet Omelette, with rum.

Boston Brown Bread, Rolled.   French Rolls.   English Muffins.

Café.

Pennant-topped Hotel Ontario and Auditorium were the park's major buildings. Housed at the right is an attraction that swept the country—LIFE MOTION PICTURES. Inside, eager patrons marveled at shaky, nickelodeon-style "flickers." Notice the white-shirted barker hawking tickets to the half-hour-long series of the Biograph Company's first moving pictures.

The poster, seen throughout the city, offered a special "augmented programme on Memorial Day." It was a time to "find forgetfulness of the anxieties and cares of these perplexing times."

This 1907 panoramic view of Ontario Beach Park shows it sparsely built. Soon the resort would be crammed with rides and other attractions. The large white structure in the foreground was the "Bromo Seltzer Tower." A stairway led to the observation tower atop the shaft where a

After the installation of the long Government Pier at Charlotte, so much sand accumulated behind it that the shore line changed at least twice. New boardwalk promenades were constructed at the park in 1896 and 1902, each closer to the advancing shoreline. In this photo, the shoreline has expanded as much as 20 to 30 feet from its original site.

spiral chute whisked one to the ground. Government Pier separated the Genesee River from the lake waters. The ferry boat *Windsor* connected the park with Summerville, a popular summer retreat across the river.

In 1894 only a few bathers ventured into Lake Ontario's shallow shore waters. When they did, both men and women were required to wear suits that covered their torsos. Few really went swimming, as can be noted by the "bather" still wearing her hat.

The "gay nineties" photo was made on Ontario Beach Park's promenade. Although it appears, at first, to be taken on a rainy day, most Victorian ladies used their parasols to protect their "peaches and cream" complexions, unlike the tan-seeking lasses of today.

West of the Scenic Railway, two 90-foot-tall poles were erected and a wire stretched between the towering poles. The year was 1895, and the attraction was the tight-rope walker known as "the Great Blondin." Climbing the pole, he carried a chair and table, a kerosene cook stove, a frying pan, and an egg. To the delight of the spectators, while atop the wire, he sat on the chair, fried the egg, and ate it. Wiping his mouth with a flourish, he proclaimed he'd just enjoyed the best well-balanced meal in the county.

Great throngs arrived at the park in 1904 to watch the free vaudeville acts. Few drew a larger crowd than the "Great Blondin," famous tight-rope walker, on his second visit to the park. He amazed his audiences with his remarkable daredevil antics atop a 90-foot-high wire.

25

Looping the Gap, Out-door Exhibition at Ontario Beach, N. Y.

Even more amazing acts were used to boost park attendance. A daredevil is "looping the cap" while riding a bicycle. Years later, the feat was repeated by a performer known as "Morok," who looped the gap while driving an early horseless carriage.

5993. Death Trap Loop, Ontario Beach Park, Charlotte, N. Y.

Perched some 50 feet in the air, an early daredevil was ready to plunge down the "Death Trap Loop" when an assistant released his bicycle. The vast crowd appeared to be holding its collective breath awaiting the outcome of the feat.

Few of the gentlemen wearing celluloid collars or the ladies in ostrich-plumed hats would soon forget the summer the Z-1129 soared over their heads, incredibly defying gravity. Created from goldbeater's skin, the gas bag was filled with hydrogen gas. The inflammable gas was generated by the chancy practice of pouring sulfuric acid into tar-lined barrels of iron scarps. The "gravity-defying" moment was frozen in time by an alert photographer.

Called the "Elevated Stage," this was where many of the free acts at the park were presented. Nearby was a generous supply of green-painted park benches to accommodate park visitors. The bicycle acrobat was determining how fresh the air might be while atop his lofty unicycle perch. (Photo courtesy Greece Historical Society.)

It was one of the last acts at the end of the season on September 8, 1917, when this bicycle acrobat performed on a swaying gridwork high above the crowds at Ontario Beach. (Photo courtesy Greece Historical Society.)

With a drum roll and a wave of the hand this high diver leaps off into space. The crowd is hushed as he plunges toward a small, water-filled tank 90 feet below. The photograph was taken August 18, 1917. (Photo courtesy Greece Historical Society.)

What better way to attract and amuse the public than a free elephant act? Atop the park's stage, the elephant pair are put through their routines. (Photo courtesy Greece Historical Society.)

As the park band played a waltz, the pachyderms swayed in time to the serenade. The small girl in the foreground seems fascinated. (Photo courtesy Greece Historical Society.)

ELEPHANTS IN BATHING AT ONTARIO BEACH.

While Ontario Beach Park hosted many unusual attractions, none drew a larger crowd than when an elephant and two elks swam and took a bath together. It was all part of publicity for an Elk's Convention and Street Fair held in Rochester in August 1899.

THE GERMAN VILLAGE AND MIDWAY.
ONTARIO BEACH PARK, N.Y.

In 1900 almost a quarter of Rochester's population spoke German or boasted German ancestry. Little wonder when, at one year's opening, visitors discovered building facades reminiscent of a German village along the midway. Schnapps, bratwurst, knockwurst, and big salty pretzels were sold there.

When few families ever traveled farther than the rails could take them, what could be more intriguing than a vicarious visit to the mysterious Orient? Opening the season as "The Garden of Gaiety," a Japanese village filled the park with patrons. The Japan Bazaar housed concessions loaded with paper parasols, tin toys, china doo-dads, and other inexpensive souvenirs. Nearby, swains and their sweethearts found the "Venetian Canals," a 1,600-foot, watery ride aboard a rustic gondola. This was even more romantic than visiting the Japanese Village.

Visiting the Japanese Village was the big attraction during the summer of 1909. Authenticity was enhanced by a neatly landscaped Japanese garden adjacent to a tea house operated by Mr. A. Ishida. Many crossed the graceful Oriental bridge built next to the tea house when it was rumored to bring good luck.

Japanese Village. Ontario Beach Park, N.Y.

A huge Torii gate greeted park patrons and provided a dramatic entrance into the Japanese Village. The tea house seen on the right was operated by kimono-clad Japanese.

SECOND
ANNUAL OUTING

MONROE
COUNTY
ASSESSORS'
ASSOCIATION

ONTARIO BEACH PARK
AUGUST 25,
1911

Many that gathered at the beach resort wore badges, pin-back buttons, or ribbons. These proudly designated their wearers as representing church picnic groups; social, political, civic, or fraternal societies; employee outings; or family reunions and picnics. Carefully preserved by its owner, this ribbon was last worn more than 80 years ago.

Charlotte on Lake Ontario — The Coney Island of Central New York

The artist used selective compression to encompass as many attractions as possible. The roller coaster is in the foreground. The House That Jack Built, a "crazy-house," shows up as a jumble of children's blocks. Near the midway is a menagerie carousel. Next is the auditorium building and beyond is the Ontario Hotel. In the background, the Livingston "hotel" is burning. The unique attraction, called Messmore's Fighting the Flames, was used to produce a dramatic fire rescue scene, all part of the park's daily entertainment.

Turn-of-the-century thrill seekers lined up to shoot down Ontario Beach's water toboggan. The ride's ad stated, "The bobbing up and down of the sled, the springing, kicking and unexpected movements of the rider, are a source of endless amusement to the bathers and the spectators. It is the latest, dizziest contrivance for the benefit of people anxious to head off the mercury in its efforts to climb clear out of the top of the thermometer."

Another heat wave in the summer of 1917 produced another crowd at Ontario Beach Park. The water slide is seen in the background. (Photo courtesy of Greece Historical Society.)

Three water toboggans, at Ontario Beach, Bartholomay's Pavilion, and Summerville, all in close proximity, were no coincidence. The water slides were manufactured locally as early as 1888 by the Herbert A. Shearer Toboggan Co. at the foot of River Street in Charlotte, New York.

Water toboggans were "all the go" in Victorian times. Their four styles included the Genesee, the Flash, the Swift, and the Lightning. This last and swiftest was erected in the park as an adjunct to healthful outdoor sports. The sleds, as they descended, on striking the water, were hurled out over the surface 60 to 70 feet.

35

It appears that this unique photo of the Hotel Ontario, taken on June 23, 1892, was timed to catch the employees of the Moneypeny Hammond Company at lunchtime. The luncheon was part of the fifth annual excursion to Ontario Beach Park by the company from Columbus, Ohio.

Half the Pleasure

OF SUMMER
IS A TRIP TO

ONTARIO
GEO. W. SWEENEY,
General Manager.
BEACH
PARK

On the
NEW YORK CENTRAL.

"AMERICA'S GREATEST
LAKE RESORT."

Special Fireworks Display
in Honor of Visiting Knights.

Don't Forget
THE LIVINGSTON,
In Rochester.

Remember
The NEW LA FAYETTE,
In Buffalo.

In 1895, when this ad was printed, general manager George Sweeney of the New York Central Railroad was modestly referring to their Ontario Beach Park creation as "America's Greatest Lake Resort." The ad was also meant to attract the Knights of Pythias, who were holding their annual convention in Rochester at the time.

Once a summer, members of Rochester's Automobile Club paraded youngsters from the orphanage in their early model automobiles to Ontario Beach for an unforgettable day of fun, food, and frolic. The autos are seen lined up between the park's gaily decorated concessions.

On Labor Day, 1919, the grand old amusement park passed into history. Only faint memorie were left, and few living today remember any of those 35 golden summers when Ontario Beac Park was considered the "Coney Island of the West." By 1923 the Ontario Hotel becam "Kenealy's at the Lake." Open June to September, it was one of four in the Kenealy Restaura chain. The fabled old hotel was razed in 1926.

Two
BARTHOLOMAY'S RESORT

BARTHOLOMAY PAVILION, AT CHARLOTTE.

In 1874 Henry Bartholomay, owner of Rochester's largest brewery, created Bartholomay Park and built a resort structure called Bartholomay Pavilion. Situated west of what would become Ontario Beach Park, it was a beer hall complete with singing waiters serving hefty 5¢ schooners of beer, dirndl-dressed lasses dispensing hot pretzels from long sticks, and a German band for singing and dancing. The Summernight Festival of the Maennerchor was an early event held there.

Cottage Hotel. Ontario Beach, N. Y., one of Rochester's beautiful suburbs on the shores of Lake Ontario.

Bartholomay's Cottage Hotel occupied a large central building and had a series of summer "cottages" attached at right angles to one another. All were tied together with wide verandas with distinctive X-braced railings.

The young girl posing in a frilly, white frock is Henrietta Present. The photo was taken by Emmett Craig. The family was well respected in Rochester.

The "cottages," a string of summer homes, were rented for the season to some of Rochester's leading families. It was a matter of some pride to spend the summer at one of the lake front cottages.

Bartholomay Park, developed prior to Ontario Beach, had its own Victorian-style pavilion. It shaded band members, was used for picnics, and served as an observation deck from which to watch yacht and sailboat races on Lake Ontario.

The pinback button was last worn in 1907. It's a good bet that the "club" members also visited Bartholomay's Pavilion before departing the park.

The interior of Bartholomay's Pavilion accommodated scores of patrons who often filled its main floor and sat on bentwood chairs crowded around many small tables. Others found room on the balcony that ringed three sides of the large beer hall. Note that in 1905, one could have "Meals To Order At All Times." The brew of course was Bartholomay's lager beer.

The artist's dramatic rendering of the Bartholomay Hotel and grounds shows it as somewhat larger than it really was. The dense grove of trees and busy carriageway was mostly artist's license. However, the impressive hotel complex was a catalyst for the future development of neighboring Ontario Beach Park by the New York Central Railroad.

The quaint trolley terminal was located on the northwest corner of Beach Avenue just off Broadway (Lake Avenue) in Charlotte. Car 31 was one of a number of new trolleys purchased in 1912 by the Rochester & Manitou Railway. (Photo courtesy Rochester Chapter NRHS.)

Manitou Beach was reached by an adventurous ride west along the shore and across a 2,000-foot trestle built over Braddocks Bay. The Grandview Beach & Manitou Trolley Line began in May 1891. The last run of the open-air trolley was on August 31, 1925.

Three
MANITOU BEACH PARK

BEAUTIFUL MANITOU BEACH.

GRAND VIEW BEACH.

CRESCENT BEACH.

ISLAND COTTAGE.

ROCHESTER, CHARLOTTE & MANITOU R.R.

Are Ideal Excursion Resorts for

Societies, Churches, Outing Clubs.

For Terms, write
GEO. L. BROWN, Sec. and Treasurer,
Rochester, Charlotte & Manitou Railway, 32 White Street,
Rochester, N. Y.   Telephone No. 4.
Charlotte, Telephone 22-M.

65

TRESTLE ON THE ROCHESTER, CHARLOTTE AND MANITOU RAILWAY.

PICNIC GROUNDS—MANITOU BEACH.

The ad and photos were part of a campaign by the Rochester, Charlotte & Manitou Railway to promote excursions to the resort hotels, located between a series of scenic ponds and Lake Ontario. Each flourished by offering unique attractions along the trolley's shoreline route.

The Manitou Trolley was a lifeline to cottage and resort hotel owners along its 8-mile route. It brought supplies to property owners, beer and ice to hotels, and whisked family picnic groups and conventioneers to four major summer resorts on the line. The company promoted business with this ditty:

At Manitou,
Where the breezes blow,
And appetites are made.
To Manitou,
The people go,
And every care doth fade.
Just take the car,
It isn't far,
And ride along the shore
The dinner there,
Is sure a "bear,"
It will make you come for more.

A cottage colony existed at Rigney's Bluff (Shoremont) near the lake end of Dewey Avenue. Large sections of the trolley's tracks were carried away at this point by a mud slide during the winter of 1907. A breakwater of concrete slabs was then constructed. Little remains today of the Manitou Beach Trolley Line but a few of those slabs.

As the little four-wheel trolley pulled into stop 21 at the Manitou Beach grounds, its patrons easily spotted the three-story Manitou Hotel on the skyline. The circular white tent in the foreground covered William J. Reis's steam-operated merry-go-round. Tents on the right and more permanent structures covered the dance hall, bath and boathouse, shooting gallery, plus stables and refreshment stands.

Manitou Beach was the site for the Monroe County Farmers' "Pioneer Picnic." Initiated in 1894, the picnic brought together old-timers and their farm families. The 1900 program included sack and running races, nail pounding, doughnut eating, wood-sawing contests, and a skiff race on Lake Ontario.

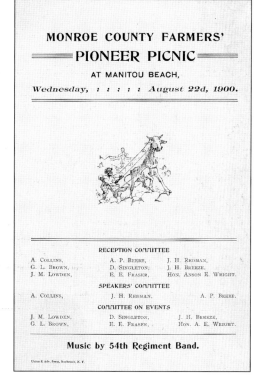

MONROE COUNTY FARMERS'
PIONEER PICNIC
AT MANITOU BEACH,
Wednesday, : : : : : August 22d, 1900.

RECEPTION COMMITTEE

A. Collins,	A. P. Beebe,	J. H. Redman,
G. L. Brown,	D. Singleton,	J. H. Breeze,
J. M. Lowden,	E. E. Fraser,	Hon. Anson E. Wright.

SPEAKERS' COMMITTEE

| A. Collins, | J. H. Redman, | A. P. Beebe. |

COMMITTEE ON EVENTS

| J. M. Lowden, | D. Singleton, | J. H. Breeze, |
| G. L. Brown, | E. E. Fraser, | Hon. A. E. Wright. |

Music by 54th Regiment Band.

Union & Adv. Press, Rochester, N. Y.

47

The 25-room Elmheart, built in 1895 by Jacob Odenbach, became a favorite summer destination for Pittsburgh businessmen whose Colony Club tents were erected nearby. Rochester girls and their beaus enjoyed six dances for a quarter at the Elmheart's popular dance hall. When the big dance bands played there, the trolley line advertised: "Persons wishing to spend an evening of unalloyed pleasures in the art of terpsicore will find Manitou an ideal place. Last car leaves (for the city) at 10:45 p.m." The Elmheart lasted longer than other hotels, but succumbed to arson on September 1, 1992.

It was a warm day on July 29, 1917, when Pittsburgh Colony Club members got off the trolley at Manitou Beach. The club spent two weeks at the resort each year. The Elmheart Hotel is at right. (Photo courtesy of Greece Historical Society.)

This photo, taken on July 4, 1918, highlighted the latest in natty swim wear at beautiful Manitou Beach. Men were still required to keep their chests modestly covered. The snappy spoke-wheeled touring car sports a pair of 48-star American flags.

The dancing, partying, and great bands attracted many of the area's lasses to the Elmheart's dance hall or the ballroom of the Manitou Beach Hotel. This trio of young ladies can't wait for the evening festivities to begin. Perhaps they each found some male companion who enjoyed ukulele music.

A grand touring car arrives at the impressive Manitou Beach Hotel. Its wide porches were favorite places for catching the lake breezes. (Photo courtesy of Greece Historical Society.)

Fred (Cop) Odenbach, owner of the Hofbrau House in Rochester, became the proprietor of the Manitou Hotel in 1904. It served outstanding cuisine into the 1950s in a dining room accommodating 500 people. Evening breezes often carried sounds of the dance band wafting across the grounds. Only memories are left of the choice meals and pleasant hours spent at the stately hotel.

Located in a beautiful lawn that slopes to the water's edge, the Hotel Manitou commands a magnificent view of Lake Ontario. A more charming spot where one may dine well and comfortably could not be found.

While enjoying the fresh lake breezes, visitors to Manitou strolled among shaded groves of trees, flower beds, and neatly laid out walkways leading to the Hotel Manitou. Looking from the verandas, visitors enjoyed fine views of Lake Ontario, its sailboats, and its schooners. The steamer *Rosalie,* which carried passengers from Manitou's pier to Ontario Beach Park and Sea Breeze, is seen here.

Manitou is but sixteen miles from Rochester, and a splendid improved State road leads directly to the Hotel. It is indeed a haven for motorists, offering first-class accommodations at the end of a delightful drive. It is also accessible by trolley.
FRED ODENBACH, Prop., Manitou Beach, Lake Ontario, N. Y.

Rochesterians were fully involved in the bicycle craze of the gay nineties. Early clubs raced everywhere in the countryside, often to meet at its lakeside resorts. Clubs included the Lakeview Wheelman, Flower City Cycle Club, Newport Cycle Club, Crescent Cycle Club, and the Seneca Wheelman. A special race meet between clubs was begun at Manitou. Over 50 uniformed high wheelman and "scorchers" on bikes pose for this exceptional photo.

A few lads, perhaps from one of the wheelmen's clubs, have stopped to quench their thirst at Manitou Beach grove. William Reis's carousel in the background was powered with a steam boiler and cable. Its music was played on a French organ using large steel cylinder rolls. In 1908 it was shipped to Island Cottage and later sent to a park in the Finger Lakes.

Sixty members of the Oak Leaf Club, most wearing white hats, held their annual outing at Manitou Beach. Fashions have changed since this photo was taken in 1932. (Photo courtesy Greece Historical Society.)

This 1914 photo shows the good ship *Arundell* boarding passengers at the Hojack Station in Charlotte. The Genesee River, like the railroad, provided a gateway to Lake Ontario's resorts. The steamer plied the lake between Rochester, Oswego, and the Thousand Islands.

Four

LAKE ONTARIO AND GENESEE RIVER ATTRACTIONS

An impressive sight at Ontario Beach Park was the graceful passage of a full-masted yacht as it glided into a Genesee River dock.

Charlotte Harbor, N.Y.

Ontario Beach Park visitors often watched lake steamers and schooners enter the Genesee River to dock at the long Government Pier.

A full-masted schooner glides out of the Genesee River, dwarfing a steamboat. The graceful vessels were a common sight in days gone by.

Steamer Rochester in Charlotte Harbor, Port of Rochester, N. Y.

A cruise on Lake Ontario to the Thousand Islands or to Niagara Falls was a popular weekend trip. The steamer *Rochester* offered very comfortable accommodations to its passengers from the turn of the century into the 1920s.

Prior to the turn of the century, side-wheeler steam boats were seen frequently. In the 1890s the *North King* made regular stops at the Charlotte, New York river docks.

Prior to its loss in 1894, a popular way to reach the Glen House Restaurant was to cruise up the Genesee River from Charlotte aboard the *City of Rochester*, the vessel seen in the background. Its captain stands on the ramp leading from the old steamboat landing up to the restaurant.

Built in 1870 to stimulate traffic on Lake Avenue's street car line, the Glen House Restaurant was a scenic dining site. Located north of the Driving Park Bridge at the head of river navigation, it stood on the west bank of the Genesee River. Patrons reached it by hydraulic elevator from Maplewood Park. Popular menu choices included pheasant in casserole and roasted wild duck. The restaurant, the first of Rochester's water-side retreats, burned down on May 4, 1894.

A colorful character in Rochester's past, Captain J.D. Scott, the "Excursion King," sold a round-trip, combination ticket. The 50¢ strip ticket was good for a complete tour from downtown Rochester to Lake Ontario and then to Irondequoit Bay and return. Three amusement parks, four resorts, and several fine hotel restaurants could be visited with such a ticket.

The *Titania* was one of several steamers in J.D. Scott's excursion-ticket fleet in 1910. Passengers aboard the steamer have taken the 5-mile lake cruise from Charlotte and are arriving at the Sea Breeze pier. The landing was just west of Irondequoit Bay.

Charlotte Harbor and Naval Reserve Station,
Rochester, N. Y.

This unusual view from the east bank of the Genesee River shows the Naval Reserve Station in the foreground. To the right across the river, pennants can be seen flying over the buildings at Ontario Beach Park.

The mighty dredge *T.A. Gillespie* was employed to remove silt from the Genesee River's bed.

The "Ontario No. 1" at her Dock, Charlotte, N. Y.

For 42 years, until 1950, the *Ontario No.1* took pleasure-seekers from Charlotte to quaint old Cobourg, Ontario. While excursionists enjoyed the trip, the crossing's main purpose was to transport coal-laden rail cars to Canada. The great white vessel docked up the Genesee River 2.5 miles south of the lake. Called Genesee Docks, the anchorage was built by the Buffalo, Rochester, & Pittsburgh Railroad. (Photo courtesy Russ Leo collection.)

The *S.S. Ontario No.1* carried up to 1,000 passengers. Her passenger deck had cabins, staterooms, a music room, dining salon, and a large parlor. The *Ontario's* stewards provided admirable food and service. Crossing from Charlotte to Cobourg, Canada, took five hours.

This 1920s vintage photo reveals that the Cobourg, Canada trip aboard the *Ontario No. 1* was a fashionable but somewhat windy way to spend a Sunday afternoon.

G 5684a. The Ferry Boat, Charlotte, N. Y.

A number of thriving summer attractions and tent communities arose just across the Genesee River from Ontario Beach Park. For 5¢ the steam-driven ferryboat *Windsor* transported fun-seeking throngs over the 500-foot river crossing.

Here is an early view of the Genesee River from the end of the pier at Charlotte. Summerville is on the left, and Ontario Beach Park is on the right.

The ferryboat *Windsor* floated its passengers across the Genesee River from Beach Avenue in Charlotte to Summerville on the river's east bank in just seven minutes. The *Windsor*, launched in 1894, made its final run in 1927.

Five
SUMMERVILLE RESORT

By 1905 Summerville attracted a number of wealthy Rochester families who built very substantial cottages at the resort. Stately poplars and elms graced the wide promenade bordering lake-side residences. The resort's five streets were named First through Fifth Streets.

The artist's birds-eye view shows the U.S. Life Saving Station in the foreground and the ferryboat *Windsor* arriving at the Summerville landing from Ontario Beach Park. In the middle ground is the octagon-shaped Summerville Gardens and Bathing Facilities on the lake shore. The electric trolley cars of the Rochester & Irondequoit Railroad can be seen in their big turning loop in the background. The little, gay-nineties community was located at a point of land where the Genesee River joined Lake Ontario on the east shore.

The U.S. Life Saving Station (now the Coast Guard) was located in Summerville. The station's first surf boat, seen in the 1904 photo, was christened the *Charlotte*. The crew's living quarters are to the right. (Photo courtesy Russ Leo Collection.)

n 1896 the Paul Boynton Shute Company constructed an eight-person boat ride that splashed iders into a basin inlet of the river. Called the "Shoot-the-Shutes," it was located south of the .ife Saving Station. It became the Summerville Shute Company the next year.

Large crowds often dined at the Summerville Garden. The octagon-shaped restaurant, also called the "Round House," was especially popular for social gatherings and wedding parties that saw the bride and groom off on their honeymoon aboard one of the large American or Canadian steamships docked nearby. An electric fountain played between the restaurant and the lake. Colored lights on the 60-foot waterspout awed the crowds with its "magical effect."

The interior photo of Summerville Garden displays its balcony dining area with a commanding view of the lake. In the Garden's center, a gushing fountain held live fish. Rumor had it that live alligators also swam in its pool. Note the Garden's promotion in the photo.

It appears that this group is having a dandy time at Summerville. The lake is in the background. One Victorian couldn't be more relaxed sitting in the shade of a pavilion with his feet propped on a rocking chair.

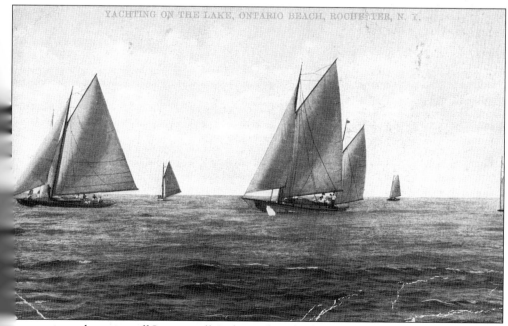

YACHTING ON THE LAKE, ONTARIO BEACH, ROCHESTER, N. Y.

nterest in yacht racing off Summerville's shores dates back prior to the 1870s.

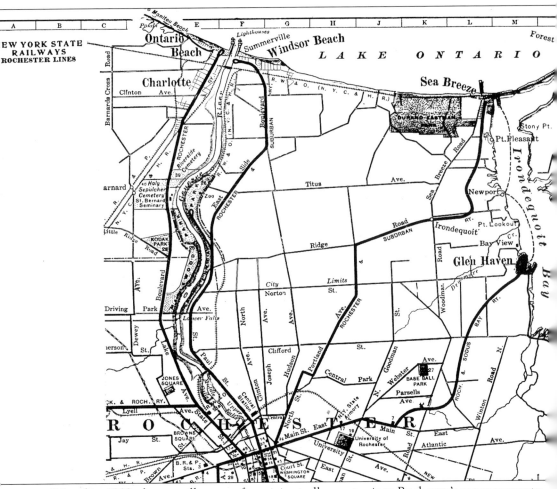

Printed in 1909, the map illustrates five major trolley routes into Rochester's summer resorts: The Rochester & Manitou Railroad to Manitou Beach, The Rochester & Lake Ontario Railroad to Ontario Beach, The Rochester & Suburban Railway to Summerville & Windsor Beach, The Rochester & Suburban Railway to Sea Breeze, The Rochester & Sodus Bay Railway to Glen Haven.

Six
WINDSOR BEACH
RESORT

oating at Windsor Beach was but one of its attractions. To many it was a great place to go
shing for the day followed by an enjoyable evening dinner around a bonfire on the beach.

The entire complement of trolley motormen and conductors were assembled for this photo. They represent the members of New York State Railway's work force that transported thousands of happy pleasure-seekers to the area's parks and resorts. (Photo courtesy of New York Museum of Transportation.)

The wet twosome was quite an attraction at Windsor Beach. These water-soaked maidens, sunning themselves on the beach, were much in evidence, greatly to the amusement of the straw-hatted and well-groomed young sports looking for smiles and nods from the pair of damsels.

On a breezy afternoon in July 1910, these maidens posed for a photo in front of a row of Windsor Beach cottages. The turned-up canoe in the background is called the "Sunny Side."

Erected in 1882, the Windsor Beach Pavilion was famous for outings, especially for those who spoke German and enjoyed brass band music. The Windsor Beach resort was located on the lake shore 1.75 miles east of Summerville and became a flourishing summer settlement by 1880.

What a fine place to dine! The picturesque Pavilion, often called the "House of Glass" due to its glass-enclosed verandas, burned on March 15, 1895, when a kerosene lamp exploded. (Photo courtesy of New York Museum of Transportation.)

Here is a seldom seen photo of the interior of the Windsor Pavilion. Japanese lanterns, bentwood chairs, and latticework made the restaurant and its polished dance floor a great place to waltz in the early 1890s. (Photo courtesy of New York Museum of Transportation.)

Hotel Windsor, Windsor Beach, N. Y., one of Rochester's beautiful suburbs, on the shores of Lake Ontar

The new Hotel Windsor soon became a beacon for the public who flocked to Windsor Beach. Built by the Rochester & Irondequoit Railroad in 1896, it replaced the Windsor Beach Pavilion. The new hotel had a board porch, dance floor, concert room, and guest rooms. Its baseball grandstand held 1,000 fans. A local historian suggests that the field's 30 electric arc lights allowed America's first night ball game to be played there!

Seven

WHITE CITY

WHITE CITY, WINDSOR BEACH, N.Y. ONE OF ROCHESTER'S BEAUTIFUL SUBURBS, ON THE SHORES OF LAKE ONTARIO.

A remarkable colony of summer folks evolved along Lake Ontario south of Windsor Beach and north of Summerville. The eight-street community was labeled White City due to the clean appearance of its white canvas tents neatly pitched in rows, each leading to the lake. Note the unique canvas rocking chair and screen door on the tent called the "Gables."

A line of shady trees border a row of summer camp tents. In this idyllic scene, residents of White City use a bench, a rocker, and a canvas camp chair on which to rest. The hammock on the right was another favorite means of relaxation.

Mom and the kids spent their entire summer under a tent at White City. After work in the steamy city, Dad took the trolley to join the family. A group of White City children have been told to hold very still for the photographer. Don't they look happy?

Summer residents of Harrison Avenue not only planted flower beds but further whitened White City by white-washing their fences and even painting tree trunks white. Strings of colorful Japanese lanterns often lit White City's streets in the evening. Out of sight were fishing poles and other bric-a-brac the campers required to spend an entire summer in their canvas "homes."

Each of White City's streets was named for an American president. In this June 1908 photo, Lincoln Avenue looks very peaceful. No horses or horseless carriages were permitted to enter the tent community. Beds of flowers have been planted down the middle of the "street."

Each season the Rochester & Pittsburgh Railroad rented narrow wooden platforms to the vacationers. The 15-feet-wide-by-60-feet-long dimensions allowed a maximum number of tent sites within the acreage they owned. Many bought their platform sites from the railroad. The Great Depression forced many to convert their summer tent frames into year-round cottages. A few of these 900-square-feet, "shotgun-style" cottages are still seen today.

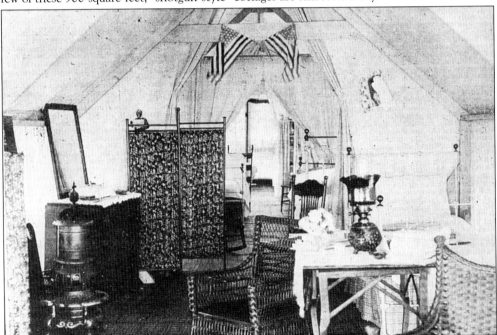

This rare photo reveals the interior of a White City "shotgun-" style tent. Note that all "rooms" are arranged directly one behind another in a straight line. The notion was that if a shotgun was fired through the front entrance the pellets would leave the rear door without hitting anything. The tent's carpeting, parlor stove, wicker chair, and iron bedsteads indicate how home-like the furnishings became.

Eight

SEA BREEZE AND BOARDWALK PARKS

168—Station and Park, SEA BREEZE.

When only a few owned horseless carriages, traction companies found it profitable to establish parks on trolley lines such as Sea Breeze. Seeking a return to nature, Victorians flocked to parks that offered a view of the water and an abundance of cooling summer breezes.

Built prior to the 1890s, Louis Geisler's Pier Restaurant rested on piers over the lake with its rear entrance bordering the Rome, Watertown, & Ogdensberg Railroad. A favored place for dining, dancing, bathing, and fishing, patrons entered under the striped awning into the Pier's popular "Wine Garden."

With the Pier Hotel in the background, three "mermaids" have left the lake for a photo. Bare legs were considered quite risque at the time.

82

View from The Bluff, Sea Breeze, N. Y.

The tracks of the Rome, Watertown, and Ogdensberg Railroad, later called the "Hojack," bridged Irondequoit Bay, preventing entrance. Steamboat excursionists were forced to cross the railroad tracks on foot, then climb a stairway up to the bluff to reach the bay or the Sea Breeze resort.

Yourself and friends are invited to attend

Geisler's Clam Bake

Sea Breeze

Sunday, August 30th, 1925

three to nine p. m.

Phone for Reservations
Suburban 5806
Suburban 7403

Valentine's Orchestra
$2.50 per plate

Louis Greisler, a well-known restauranteur, celebrated his season's closing with an invitational clambake. Greisler was proud of his world championship in the art of bag punching. His off season was spent performing on vaudeville circuits throughout the country.

Judging from the way the damsel and gentlemen are holding on to their hats, the lake breeze at Sea Breeze was pretty strong. These merrymakers are on the porch of Greisler's Pier Hotel on a windy day in 1910.

The Buffalo, Rochester, & Pittsburgh Railway advertised the annual "basket picnic" to Sea Breeze for the Sunday school classes of LeRoy. The round-trip fare seemed reasonable even for 1905; it cost just 75¢ for adults and 40¢ for little Sunday-schoolers.

The Rochester & Lake Ontario Railway, also called the "Bay Line," started carrying picnickers to Irondequoit Bay resorts as early as 1879. A frame was constructed around the little steam engine in hopes that the locomotive wouldn't scare any horses. Riders referred to it as the "dummy" engine.

Eventually the railroad was replaced with an electric trolley line. The trolley cars of the Rochester & Lake Ontario Railroad can be seen in the upper right.

Sea Breeze, One of Rochester's beautiful Summer Resorts

The trolley line continued to develop and expand its breezy picnic and recreational site to over 50 acres. Broad, graveled walkways, flower and shrub plantings, and sweeping lawns appealed to those enjoying a Sunday stroll in the 1890s.

Station and Pavilion in the Park at Sea Breeze, N.Y.

Dated July 13, 1909, from a lady named Violet to her boyfriend, this postcard reads as follows: "Having a grand time . . . XXXXX." The Rochester & Lake Ontario Railway trolley station and the Sea Breeze Pavilion, a favorite destination for picnickers, is seen in all its Victorian splendor.

Not all of the Sea Breeze resort's 50 acres were grass covered. Groves of shady trees with picnic tables and refreshment stands were a part of the attraction of Sea Breeze. For many years, the area was popularly known as "The Grove."

The unofficial "mayor" of the Grove was Emil Bueler. His birthday celebration in 1892 was held at his Sea Breeze Grove Hotel. There's little doubt of the heritage of the very Prussian-appearing gentleman hosting the party. What ethnic refreshments were on the party menu?

Yourself and friends are invited to attend the

Birthday ○ Celebration

. . OF . .

EMIL BUELER,

Thursday, August 18th, 1892,

at Sea Breeze Grove.

CLAM CHOWDER.
MUSIC IN ATTENDANCE.

EMIL BUELER.

After crossing the R.,W.,& O. Railroad tracks, paths led in two directions. One led to the bay, and the other led up a set of stairs to the Pavilion at Sea Breeze. Within the building, those seeking rest from their climb found a large, pavilion-like dining area for relaxation and refreshment. Note the framework of the "Circle Swing" on the left. The chair swing was the first amusement ride of its kind in western New York. After sunset, visitors were fascinated by the strings of electric lights strung on the swing's cables.

The sign on the Pavilion reads, "American Brew Co. Beer." The beverage and sausage hall was a stopover for many who were going on to attractions along Irondequoit Bay. The ringing of a large, school-sized bell or the clanging of a smaller bell aboard a naphtha launch alerted party-goers that their vessel was ready to depart.

A 1920s aerial view of Sea Breeze reveals its development into a full-fledged amusement park. Called the "Jack Rabbit," the roller coaster was built in 1925. Near the top of the photo is "Danceland's" domed roof. Beyond, an Olympic-sized swimming pool is seen.

This overhead photo allows one to see a number of attractions at Sea Breeze: the Old Mill and roller coaster on the left, the Caterpillar on the right, and the ride with planes suspended from the tall pylon in the background. (Photo courtesy of Irondequoit Historical Society.)

Built in 1915 at the Philadelphia Toboggan Factory and installed in 1926, the Sea Breeze carousel (Philadelphia Toboggan Company's #36) was a local landmark. The vintage merry-go-round eventually became the park's oldest ride. While newer rides were more frenetic, many young and young at heart measured their summers by a ride on that marvelous machine. Fire destroyed the priceless ride on March 31, 1994. Only 60 such grand park carousels are left in the nation.

Wonderful musical melodies accompanied the carousel's whirling ride. Sentimental sounds still echo in our ears as we recall their magical spell. Produced on an irreplaceable 1926 Wurlitzer Military Band Organ #165, the organ had "Cheerful Melodies" emblazoned across its lower section.

Taken prior to the disastrous March 31, 1994 carousel fire, this photo shows the special wood lathe used by the Philadelphia Toboggan Company to rough out the heads and bodies of its carousel horses. A completed horse awaits its first rider.

George W. Long, who bought Ontario Beach Park in 1946, had these horses on display in his carousel. They were used to illustrate the sequence of carving needed to bring a carousel horse to "life."

The youngsters in this 1927 photo have mixed emotions as they wait to be pulled to the top of the high rise that will propel them speeding and lurching through the Jack Rabbit's breath-taking twists and turns. (Photo courtesy of New York Museum of Transportation.)

The Jack Rabbit roller coaster was built by the Philadelphia Toboggan Company in Germantown, Pennsylvania, and assembled at Sea Breeze. The old grove of trees the coaster was built through was cleared long ago for additional attractions. (Photo courtesy of New York Museum of Transportation.)

"Smiling Pete" would be only too happy to "Guess your weight sonny? . . . For just one thin dime . . ., the tenth of a dollar . . ., Step right up folks . . . don't be bashful!" Pete was an institution one summer at his booth, which was located outside the carousel. (Photo courtesy of Irondequoit Historical Society.)

It was only 5¢ for a long journey on this round-about ride. In the 1920s, when this photo was captured, there were still plenty of shady trees at Sea Breeze. (Photo courtesy of Irondequoit Historical Society.)

The roller coaster and refreshment kiosk is in the foreground. Beyond it is the midway concession arcade and outdoor performance stage on the right. (Photo courtesy of Irondequoit Historical Society.)

This late 1920s photo shows Danceland, built in the heyday of the popular big dance bands. The Sea Breeze grove, once filled with Victorian picnic parties, was cleared to make room for the huge hall. (Photo courtesy of New York Museum of Transportation.)

The great, mirrored ball slowly twirled sending its sparkling lights over scores of couples dancing under the great curved dome of Danceland. While the stage appears small, the pulsing musical rhythms of bands drew hundreds to dance around the spacious hall. (Photo courtesy of New York Museum of Transportation.)

On July 1, 1925, New York State Railways, operator of the trolley line to Sea Breeze, opened the "Natatorium," the world's largest saltwater swimming pool. The 125-by-300-foot pool held filtered water with a salinity matching that of the ocean.

Where 𝒶 Is Ideal

The Ultra Violet Ray Sterilizer

The water in the Rochester Natatorium is completely re-sterilized three times each day. The three 4-lamp units have a capacity of sterilizing 4,200 gallons per minute. The manufacturer guarantees them to bring the water within the U. S. Government requirements for drinking purposes. The Ultra Violet Ray system is recognized by leading bacteriologists as the most effective and dependable method of freeing water of disease germs, especially the dreaded typhoid

The Graver Filters

There are five filters 20 ft. long by 6 ft. dia., each of which is capable of filtering 1,725 gallons per minute. This is sufficient filtration capacity for a city of 20,000 population and was installed in the Rochester Natatorium to assure absolute clarity of the water.

Laundry

Complete and modern equipment such as is used in Hotels and Laundries has been installed at the Natatorium. The suits and towels are sterilized in high-pressure live steam. The most fastidious person need have no qualms about

The enormous Natatorium boasted many amenities. The salty water was heated to 75 degrees and sterilized at a rate of 4,200 gallons per minute. There was a high dive tower, water toboggan, and water merry-go-round. Around the pool-side, promenade grandstands served crowds for water ballet and swim meets, a bandstand for roaring twenties bands, a barber shop, and a dining room. Gone by 1931, it sure made a great splash in its day.

It was Bert Wilson, traffic manager for the New York State Railway, who dreamed up the idea of the huge Natatorium. The opportunity to swim in salty ocean water had a lot of appeal to local folks who lived far from the ocean. Water depth under the diving tower was 10 feet. (Photo courtesy of New York Museum of Transportation.)

George Carpenter, pool manager, appears to be much appreciated by his quartet of adoring bathing beauties. (Photo courtesy of New York Museum of Transportation.)

What a great time the kids are having on the water merry-go-round. The stage was used for concerts and music for water ballet performances. (Photo courtesy of New York Museum of Transportation.)

One of the attractions at the Natatorium was the bevy of bathing beauties that performed there. The bathing suits in this June 12, 1932 photo are a far cry from the ones worn just a few years earlier. The Natatorium closed May 24, 1931. (Photo courtesy of New York Museum of Transportation.)

The happy expressions on the faces of the lady employees of the Sherwood Shoe Factory indicate that they're enjoying their picnic at Sea Breeze. Taken *c.* 1915, the photo also shows two very pleased gentlemen.

Few remember Boardwalk Park, located below Sea Breeze and north of Culver Road along the lake shore. Boats reached it at its two long lake piers. Some may recall the Ferris wheel, merry-go-round, and shooting gallery or playing bingo, "skee-roll," or "pokerino" at the tiny amusement center. Very few may even remember when it was called Karnival Kourt.

A long line of fun seekers are ready to board the steamer at the Boardwalk Park's long pier. Steamer tickets were available from the booth on the pier. (Photo courtesy of Greece Historical Society.)

As shown, Sea Breeze offered pony rides. The Positype Studio concession recorded the scene. The young riders look happy, but the ponies appear resigned.

The Bonekessel family ran the concessions at Boardwalk Park. Even in the 1920s when this photo was taken, parking was at a premium. Many parked at Sea Breeze and made their way downhill to Boardwalk Park. (Photo courtesy of Greece Historical Society.)

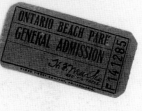

Long ago, some folks saved their Boardwalk coupons and tickets related to Ontario Beach Park. It's amazing that these fragile, but tangible tokens of the past, have made it through the funnel of time.

Rochester Canoe Club, Irondequoit Bay, N.Y.

Many private cottages were built along the west side of the bay. Several were owned by social and sporting groups such as the Rochester Canoe Club (left). The Onoko Club cottage is on the right. Founded in 1882, the Canoe Club had a "war canoe" called *Huff*. Constructed by the Captain George Ruggles, who was noted for his racing canoes and other inventions, the canoe had brightly colored sails trimmed with Seneca Indian designs.

The white-capped trio of "sailors" were members of the Rochester Canoe Club. Their club house, just across an inlet bridge north of the Newport House, made it convenient for members to obtain any liquid libation they might have required.

Nine

IRONDEQUOIT
BAY RESORTS

While Manitou Beach and Ontario Beach lured great hoards of vacationers from distant villages and cities, many Rochesterians preferred the relative tranquility of Irondequoit Bay and its attractions. Access to cottages and hotels was by trolley from Rochester, steamboat from Charlotte, or a naphtha launch from the mouth of the bay.

Eagerly looked forward to each autumn was the annual Fall Regatta and Clam Bake. Hosted by the Rochester Canoe Club, it was one of the social highlights of the season. The clam pit opened at 5 p.m. and was followed by an evening of dancing, which commenced at 8 p.m.

Seventy members of one bayside group, the Birds and Worms Club, established their society "for the protection of fish and game, and to enhance game laws of the state." In its first year, the club began an annual Calico Ball for charitable as well as social purposes. Several hundred invitees often attended the ball.

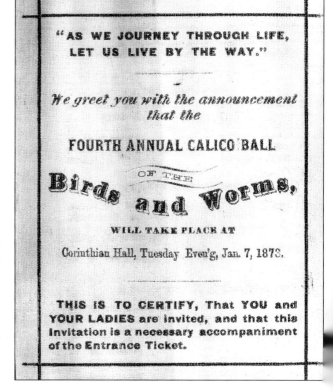

"AS WE JOURNEY THROUGH LIFE, LET US LIVE BY THE WAY."

We greet you with the announcement that the

FOURTH ANNUAL CALICO BALL

Birds and Worms,

OF THE

WILL TAKE PLACE AT

Corinthian Hall, Tuesday Even'g, Jan. 7, 1873.

THIS IS TO CERTIFY, That YOU and YOUR LADIES are invited, and that this invitation is a necessary accompaniment of the Entrance Ticket.

About 1910 the landing at Irondequoit Bay's mouth was so clogged with reedy cattails that in some places only a narrow channel provided access to the upper bay's resort attractions. Fishermen often caught carp and huge mud turtles that lived in this marshy area.

1019 THE MARSHES, IRONDEQUOIT BAY.

The boats that plied the bay were small, built on the bay, and served its summer resorts from *c.* 1875 until the 1920s. As can be seen in the photo, small launches could more easily navigate around the bog-like area of Irondequoit Bay known as the "Marshes."

This 1890s photo takes one back to a time when folks existed happily without cabin cruisers, jet skis, or pontoon party boats. However, getting supplies to the cottage might have been a problem. (Photo courtesy of Irondequoit Historical Society.)

Weeping willows shaded these summer cottages at the bay. It was an era when life moved at a more leisurely pace. There was little road rage when you drove buggies such as these. (Photo courtesy of Irondequoit Historical Society.)

Cottage owners, conoeists, boaters, swimmers, and resort visitors all enjoyed the tranquil waters of Irondequoit Bay. The sheltered bay is still a magnet for sailing, fishing, and other water-related activities.

At a bayside cottage named "Dolphy," a proud crew of summer sailors pose for their photograph. The vintage bicycle in front of the sailboat Dolphy looks new.

The Point Pleasant hostelry, erected in 1897 "on picturesque Irondequoit Bay," was perched halfway up a bluff. In the 1930s, Louis V. Rund ran the hotel, which was noted for its clambakes. The venerable landmark burned on a cold day in December 1954.

View from Point Pleasant, Irondequoit Bay, near Rochester, N. Y.

Viewing from the Point Pleasant Hotel, one easily spotted the bay's more celebrated cottages. The Early Birds and Unfortunate Worms was a sportsmen's club formed in 1870. The fraternity of hunters and fishermen built their clubhouse in 1872, just south of Point Pleasant. Today the club's 5 acres are the site of the Newport Yacht Club.

Posed for their annual group photograph are Karle Lithographic Manufacturing Company employees. The photo was part of the firm's 1909 outing at Bay View. Unlike many pictures of men taken during this era, all but one gentleman has removed his hat.

Irondequoit Bay's resorts and cottage retreats were favorite spots where the more unique local groups kicked up their heels. One group of young rowdies was the Burn Up Sky Fire Association. One can be sure their annual picnic in 1902 at Glen Edith was a memorable one.

The *Glen Edyth*, one of the naphtha launches that transported summer folks around the bay, was built by Orlo Walzo and Valentine Shaefer *c.* 1908. The tattered photo of the builders and their boat reportedly came from the wall of Glen Edyth's saloon.

Covered with vines and shaded by tall willows swaying in the bay breeze, the Newport House attracted people in several ways: some by steamer, some by horse and buggy, and others by trolley. Visitors rented boats, played baseball, pitched horse shoes, and enjoyed picnics. Others stayed at Newport and appreciated clean accommodations while savoring elaborate dinners.

Large assemblies of local societies held their annual gatherings at the Newport House. A crowd congregated on the baseball diamond and witnessed a series of races, games, and contests.

The Newport House became the oldest resort on the bay, outlasting all its competition. For a score of years, Monroe County supervisors held a picnic there while formulating the political future for its leaders. Today, guests still arrive to discover a rebuilt Newport House and restaurant, a pub and cafe, and an extensive marina.

In 1840 Joseph Vinton converted his shingle mill into a gin mill. In 1842 it became the Newport House, a bayside retreat attracting an aristocratic clientele with its fine dining and combination two-story pavilion and steamboat dock. The double-decker pavilion was a most refreshing location on a lazy summer day.

Rochester had a score of shoe factories between 1865 and 1935. In 1886 the E.P. Reed employees were treated to the annual company "pic-nic" at the Newport House. The ribbon an employee wore that day became a cherished keepsake for many years.

This 1909 photo provides us with a marvelous look into yesterday's Victorian era. Note the faces, hairdos, and dress of the throng gathered at the Newport House for their annual Sunday school picnic. The photo once belonged to Mrs. August Panneitz of Weeger Street.

For many years, the Monroe County supervisors and ex-supervisors made the Newport House the site for their annual meeting. President Joseph H. Sherman of Rush, New York, presided at the 1906 gathering that included reports, a formal ball and reception, contests for the kids, and awards for the eldest members present. Also scheduled was "a cakewalk on the green by local artists."

Ten

GLEN HAVEN PARK

With the bay in the background, this bird's-eye view reveals early Glen Haven Park. Built in 1879, the Griebels Hotel was the first resort at Glen Haven. The Glen Haven Hotel, at left, followed in 1880. Here, two trolley cars of the Irondequoit Park Railroad Company have disembarked their passengers. A steam-driven carousel rests under the conical tent in the center of this 1896 photo.

5675   Glen Haven near Rochester, N. Y.

Received you postal all O. K. How is the amusm getting along. Russell

Dated 1908, this scene shows Glen Haven's pony ride in the left foreground. The Glen Haven Hotel and tent-covered carousel are nearly obscured by trees.

The steam launch *Glen Haven* is crawling into the pier at Glen Haven Park. It seems unbelievable that 15,000 visitors were an average weekend crowd at the amusement park.

Prior to air conditioning, great hoards of sweltering Rochesterians and suburbanites sought relief by escaping to the cool breezes at Ontario Lake or Irondequoit Bay. A group from Glen Haven is boarding the launch *Sea Breeze* for a trip to another bayside resort.

Looking South toward Newport and Glen Haven, from summer home of Wm. H. Burr, 160 ft. above water, Irondequoit Bay, N. Y.

While many pleasure seekers used the trolley to reach Glen Haven, others enjoyed the natural beauty of the bay as they flowed through scenic waters in an open launch. Summer cottages and resort hotels were built at each of the points along the bay.

An August 1907 issue of *Trolley Topics* informs the reader that "Glen Haven Park is now in the height of its glory. It is the one favored spot of Rochester's vast army of amusement lovers. Always something to enthuse or amuse; never a dull moment in this picturesque garden of Nature. Free admission, free seats, free vaudeville and a good time for everybody." The park's tree-lined promenade is shown here.

The hillside behind Glen Haven was both steep and woodsy. Two Victorian couples, dressed in their Sunday finest, posed for this picture. An early photographer captured the moment for future posterity.

This 1908 photo reveals that Glen Haven's amusement area is now called Dreamland, and the park entrance now abuts the trolley loop. The 6-mile ride from Rochester's Four Corners took under 30 minutes. The 32-seat trolleys left for the park at 20-minute intervals. Fare was 20¢ for a round-trip ticket.

Every few years the entrance facade to Glen Haven was rebuilt. The Irondequoit Park trolley disembarked its passengers, who were eager, perhaps, to watch the 3:30 p.m. vaudeville show. A long line of joined concession stands are seen in the background.

Taken from the bluff above the park in 1908, the scene focuses on the huge, red-roofed pavilion protecting Glen Haven's menagerie-style carousel. Within, merry-go-round riders whirled to the stirring notes of John Philip Sousa's "Stars and Stripes Forever," which resounded from an ornate band organ.

Not unlike today's space liftoffs, were the astounding balloon ascensions of yesterday. A huge throng in 1904 circled Glen Haven's baseball field to witness the huge balloon drift upward. Rochester's Thomas P. Dunn, originator of Sen-Sen, placed his ad for the 5¢ "Throat Ease & Breath Perfume," on the balloon's side.

Glen Haven Park, called Dreamland, attracted the masses with its mammoth "Circus Maximus" stage. Measuring 30 feet deep and 60 feet long, the stage could accommodate sizable performances. (Photo courtesy of Irondequoit Historical Society.)

When Henry Reuther managed the Glen Haven Hotel between 1888 and 1910, no other hotel came close in popularity. Elegant dinners were served on its wide verandas. Its headwaiter, Englishman "Fritz" Waltz, was famous for having served Queen Victoria on more than one occasion. Following dinner, Theodore Dossenbach's orchestra played while cuddling twosomes glided gracefully over the highly polished dance floor. This was all part of life in the gay nineties.

This 1890 photo looks south from Glen Haven toward Schneider's Island Hotel, which was built in 1877. By this time, 16 bay resort hotels catered to hungry Victorians, serving them a variety of food and drink. The wooden derrick raft was used to drill for fresh water.

Newly planted trees, a new lawn, and wide wooden walkways encouraged patronage at the Bay View Hotel. The side-wheel steamer *Norman H. Galusha,* anchored on Irondequoit Bay, awaits boarders. Shown in the center is the naphtha launch *Island Queen* moored at the Old White House Hotel north of Bay View.

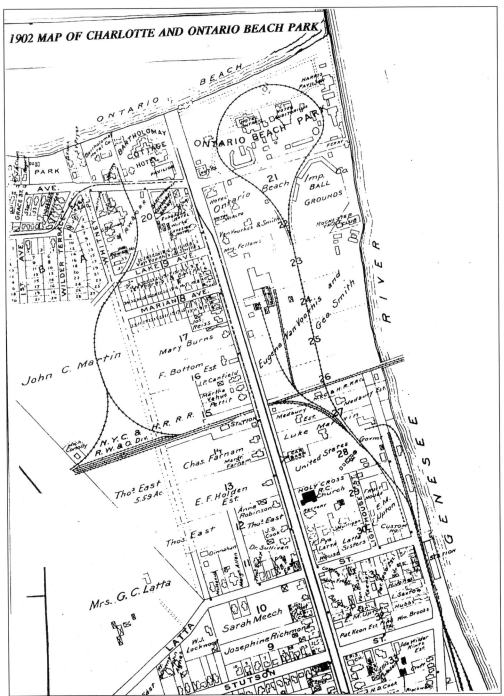

This turn-of-the-century map is useful for orientation to Charlotte and the area around Ontario Beach Park.